Sing a Song of People

by Lois Lenski

Illustrated by Giles Laroche

HAMPTON-BROWN

Illustrations copyright © 1987 by Giles Laroche. Text copyright
© 1965 by The Lois Lenski Covey Foundation, Inc. This edition
published by arrangement with Little, Brown and Company, Inc.
and The Lois Lenski Covey Foundation, Inc.

The text of "Sing a Song of People" first appeared in *The Life I Live*
by Lois Lenski, and is reprinted here by arrangement with The Lois
Lenski Covey Foundation, Inc.

Hampton-Brown
P.O. Box 223220
Carmel, California 93922
800-333-3510
www.hampton-brown.com

Printed in the United States of America.

ISBN 0-7362-1895-5

03 04 05 06 07 08 09 10 11 12 10 9 8 7 6 5 4 3 2 1

For Andrea and Beth

Sing a song of people
Walking fast or slow;

People in the city,
Up and down they go.

People on the sidewalk,

People on the bus;

People passing, passing,

In back and front of us.

People on the subway
Underneath the ground;

People riding taxis
Round and round and round.

People with their hats on,

Going in the doors;

People with umbrellas
When it rains and pours.

People in tall buildings

And in stores below;

Riding in elevators
Up and down they go.

People walking singly,

People in a crowd;

People saying nothing,
People talking loud.

People laughing, smiling,

Grumpy people too;

People who just hurry
And never look at you!

Sing a song of people
Who like to come and go;

Sing of city people
You see but never know!